BIBLE I

Simply Explained

By
B. A. RAMSBOTTOM

GOSPEL STANDARD TRUST PUBLICATIONS
1995
12(b) Roundwood Lane, Harpenden,
Herts. AL5 3DD, England.

© Gospel Standard Trust Publications 1986

ISBN 0 903556 77 4

1st Printing 1984
2nd Printing 1986
3rd Printing 1986
4th Printing 1988
5th Printing 1992
6th Printing 1995

Printed in Great Britain
by Elphick Colour Print

Cover illustration by Philip Lewis

CONTENTS

INTRODUCTION

Some years ago two small Irish children were left orphans, and the Roman Catholics tried to take them into one of their schools. The little children did not want to go, saying that they were not Roman Catholics. In the end the matter came before a judge, and in court they were asked dozens of questions about what they believed. *They could answer them all.* The judge (and I think he was a Roman Catholic) had to say, 'Well, these children know what they believe, and no one can shake them out of it, that they are Protestants.'

For a long time it has been my desire that our children should know what we believe. The Roman Catholics know their doctrines. The Jehovah's Witnesses know theirs. May our children not be in any doubt as to what is the truth. So many know all the Bible stories, but not the precious doctrines of our most holy faith.

The chapters of this book originated in a series of talks on 'what we believe' given in the Sabbath school at the chapel where I am pastor. The children were aged from seven to sixteen, and in most cases seemed to have little difficulty in understanding. Most interesting were some of the deep doctrinal questions which even some of the little ones asked afterwards.

We realize that it is easier for children to understand something explained to them personally than to read it from a book. With younger children it would be helpful if the chapters were read to them.

God's promise is: 'This shall be written for the generation to come: and the people which shall be created shall praise the Lord.'

We have been encouraged to press on with this publication believing that there is nothing of this nature in print, and yet such a crying need.

A few things should be borne in mind in reading the book:

1. The children to whom the addresses were first given all had a general background knowledge of the stories of the Bible.

2. Obviously much more could have been said and many more things dealt with—but the desire was to keep the chapters simple.

3. The author writes as a convinced Strict Baptist but the doctrines are those held by all who believe the Reformed faith, commonly called Calvinism.

4. The various stories that are told are given as the author remembers hearing or reading them. It has been impossible to check the accuracy of each detail.

5. At the end of each chapter there are one or two suggested Scripture passages. These are not intended as 'proof texts' but rather as helpful Bible readings on the subject.

6. While the title is 'Bible Doctrines Simply Explained', the author fully realizes that it is only the meaning that can be explained. A true, spiritual understanding must come through the teaching of the Holy Spirit in the heart.

CHAPTER 1

GOD

Many years ago an old man lay ill in bed. He was a wicked old man who did not believe in God. Over his bed he had written 'GOD IS NOWHERE'.

One day his little granddaughter came into the bedroom to see him. She was just learning to read so he asked her to try to read what was written over the bed. Slowly she began, and what she read was this: 'GOD . . . IS . . . NOW . . . HERE.' *God is now here!*

The old man trembled. For the first time he realized that there *is* a God.

The first thing in religion is 'I believe in God'.

How do we know about God?

The Bible tells us (Romans 1: 20) that even by looking at the beautiful things that God has made we may know there is a God. The running streams, the beautiful sunset, the sea, the sky, the stars, the mighty mountains and hills—in all we can see that there is a God. All cry out, 'There is a God, and He made us!'

But it is in the Bible that we really learn about God. Who is God? What is He like? Are there more Gods than one? The Bible gives us all these answers.

One God

You will have heard at school of how the Greeks and Romans, the Anglo-Saxons, and the Vikings believed in all sorts of gods—Mars, Jupiter, Mercury, Diana, Thor,

Woden: men gods and women gods, gods of war, gods of love, gods of all kinds of things. The Bible tells us there is *only one true and living God.* All the others are false gods, dead gods. Our God sees. He hears. He speaks. He knows. He is the living God.

What is God like?

I asked a group of children to find out as many words as they could to describe God—so that, from the Bible, we could find out what He is like. Very quickly we found the following:

God is holy, pure, and righteous. He hates sin.

God is almighty. He can do anything. He can do everything. (Of course, the old Puritans used to say, 'God can't *die* or *lie*'.)

God is eternal. You know the story of Moses and the burning bush. There God told Moses His name is 'I AM'. Only God can always say that. A hundred years ago you and I could not say, 'I am'. In another hundred years, you and I will not be able to say, 'I am'.

God is immutable. This may seem a hard word. Why not just say that God does not change, He is unchanging? Because immutable means more than that. It means that God *cannot* change.

God is invisible. We cannot see Him, but He can always see us. Think of the little children's hymn:

> God is in heaven. Can He see
> When I am doing wrong?
> Yes, that He can: He looks at me
> All day and all night long.

God is love. God is merciful. God is wise. God is gracious.

Where is God?

Once I asked a group of children this question: Where is God? Three hands went up, and there were three different answers. *But all were right*.

'God is in heaven.'

'God is everywhere.'

'God is here.'

The Trinity

You girls and boys will have heard people speak of 'the Trinity'. What does it mean?

The Bible teaches us that there is only one God, but there are three Persons in that one God—the Father, the Son, and the Holy Ghost.

God the Father is God.

God the Son (the Lord Jesus Christ) is God.

God the Holy Spirit is God.

People have tried to explain the Trinity, but no one can ever explain it. There is a story that years ago a minister said to his morning congregation that in the evening he would 'explain the Trinity'. That afternoon he saw one of his old deacons kneeling by the river with a spoon in his hand. 'Whatever are you doing?' he asked.

'Emptying the river with the spoon,' was the reply.

'You can never do it.'

'I shall do it as well as you can explain the Trinity this evening!' said the wise old man.

But though we cannot explain it or understand it, we

must believe it. People *have* tried to explain it. The reason the Irish have the little three-leaved shamrock for their emblem is because Patrick (usually known as St Patrick) when asked about the Trinity plucked a shamrock and said, 'Three in one'. Three leaves; one shamrock. Some have said our finger is bone, blood, and skin. The Puritans spoke of the sun, its beams, and its heat. But none *really* can explain the Trinity. It is a mystery—yet a mystery told to us in the Bible.

There are many things I cannot understand and yet I most firmly believe. I firmly believe that when I press the light switch, a light will come on in the bulb in the ceiling. I know it. I am sure of it. But I am no electrician; I cannot explain it.

How then can we think of the Trinity? Well, whenever Father, Son, or Holy Ghost are mentioned, each one is described as God—yet still the Bible says, 'Only one God'.

Then the three are joined together as being equal. Perhaps the text repeated more than anything else is 'the benediction'. You hear it at the end of every service. Here all three Persons are joined together as one God: 'The grace of our Lord Jesus Christ, and the love of God [that is, the Father], and the communion of the Holy Ghost, be with you all' (2 Corinthians 13: 14).

Also when a person is baptized he is baptized 'in the name (one name) of the Father, and of the Son, and of the Holy Ghost' (Matthew 28: 19).

But perhaps the most helpful for children is the account of when Jesus was baptized in the river Jordan. There was God the Son in the water. God the Holy Ghost could be seen coming down like a dove from heaven. God the Father's voice could be heard speaking: 'This is My beloved Son.' Three Persons, one God. In the early days of the Christian church there was a saying: 'Would you know the Trinity? Then go to the river Jordan.'

The wonderful thing is that the great, holy God makes Himself known to men and women, boys and girls. He makes Himself known in the Lord Jesus. Until He makes Himself known all is a mystery. A mystery is something that cannot be known until it is shown to us.

If a golden cup were hidden in your house, what it was and where it was would be a mystery. But if the person who hid it should pull up the loose boards in your bedroom floor and take that cup, and show it to you, even *give* it to you, then the *mystery* would be *revealed*.

We need to pray: 'Lord, reveal Thyself to me.'

The wisest cannot know it without it being revealed. The simplest can if it is revealed. Was it not a complete idiot boy, who hardly spoke all his life, who before he died said, 'What can I see? What can I see? I can see One, and the One is Three. Three-in-one and One-in-three! And all the Three are all for me'?

Suggested Bible readings

Psalm 104 (especially the first few verses). There are other similar Psalms.

Isaiah 6.

Isaiah 40 (especially verses 12 to 26).

Matthew 3: 13–17.

CHAPTER 2

THE BIBLE

The Bible is God's book. It tells us all about God. It is true from beginning to end. When you have a textbook at school (say chemistry or history) you do not want any mistakes in it.

We say that the Bible is *inspired.* 'All Scripture is given by inspiration of God' (2 Timothy 3: 16). What do we mean? We do not just mean what people mean when they say of a boy in a race, 'He ran like someone inspired.' We mean much more than this. We mean GOD-BREATHED. God breathed out the Bible.

Different men wrote—Moses, Samuel, David, Isaiah, Matthew, Mark, Luke, John, Paul, and others. They wrote over hundreds of years. Some were very clever; some were simple men. But their words all agree. They claim special authority for themselves.

We are told that 'holy men of old spake as they were moved by the Holy Ghost' (2 Peter 1: 21). The word 'moved' is the word used for a ship being carried along before the wind. Peter well knew how the ships were moved on the Sea of Galilee; and he uses the very same word for how he (and the other writers) were *moved* by God.

God did not use the writers of the Bible just like a boy or girl may use a typewriter. The typewriter does not know or feel anything. The writers felt what they wrote, and Paul does not write like Peter, or Peter like John. But God saw that the very words He wanted to be written were used.

We also use the word *infallible*. That means more than saying the Bible is true. It means that there just cannot be anything wrong in the Bible (though, of course, there are things we cannot understand).

You will often hear people saying the Bible is not true. Perhaps a teacher at school, or a friend. But it is very, very important that we hold fast to the truth of the Bible. Really it is as simple as this: *If God has been kind enough to give us a book about Himself, He will make sure there are no mistakes in it.*

People so often will talk about contradictions in the Bible. They say, 'One place says this and another place says something quite different.'

Let me illustrate by a story. In the early years of my pastorate two teenage girls from chapel both sent me a postcard. They were on holiday together, staying in the same place. The postcards were written the same day, posted the same day, and arrived together. One said, 'It is a most beautiful day. The sun is shining.' The other said, 'It is raining.' They were both honest girls. Why did they write different things, and yet both told the truth? No doubt you can think of lots of answers. So it is with God's Word.

Have you noticed how the Lord Jesus always spoke so reverently of the Bible? He said, 'The Scripture cannot be broken' (John 10: 35). When He first preached He quoted from the Bible to introduce Himself (Luke 4: 16–21). When He fought Satan He used the Bible as His weapon (Luke 4: 1–12). He quoted the Bible to teach His hearers (John 6: 25–34) and to silence His enemies (Matthew 15: 1–9). Even on the cross the Lord Jesus quoted Scripture (Matthew 27: 46). And when He was risen from the dead He still spoke of the Old Testament Scriptures (Luke 24: 27).

Probably the kind of things that people at school tell you they do not believe are about Adam and Eve, about Noah and his ark, about Lot's wife being turned into a pillar of salt, or about Jonah and the whale. It is very interesting that Jesus Himself picked out all these stories and referred to them as being true! (Matthew 19: 4, 5; Luke 17: 26, 27; Luke 10: 12; Matthew 12: 39–41.)

Some girls and boys will ask: 'What is the Apocrypha?' The Apocrypha is a number of old books from Bible days which have never really been counted as part of the Bible. Our Bible consists of the thirty-nine books of the Old Testament and the twenty-seven books of the New. You will notice that often in the New Testament the Old is quoted with 'God said', or, 'The Holy Ghost said', but never is the Apocrypha quoted.

Our Bible was, of course, first written in Hebrew and Greek, but we thank God for a good translation. Many children will have read of how William Tyndale spent hours turning the Bible into English. He said he wanted the most ignorant ploughboy to be able to understand the Bible as much as a learned man. How wonderful to think of the love of this man, hidden away year after year in an attic, working day and night that we might have our English Bible! And at last he was caught, strangled, and burned. It is one thing to be a famous preacher with hundreds listening, and another to be shut away in secret, wearily translating.

We thank God for our Bible in English. We think of the days when a farmer gave a whole cart-load of hay to buy one page of the Bible!

We have heard of some people who would fight until death for the fact that the Bible is true. *But they never read it!*

A little girl had a Bible given to her. She wrote at the front:

> Divine Instructor! gracious Lord!
>   Be Thou for ever near;
> Teach me to love Thy sacred Word,
>   And find the Saviour there.

And she did find the Saviour there. May we read it, and love it, and above all, find the Lord Jesus there.

That is a good prayer in reading the Bible: 'Open Thou mine eyes that I may behold wondrous things out of Thy law' (Psalm 119: 18).

Suggested Bible readings
  Psalm 19.
  Any part or all of Psalm 119.

CHAPTER 3

CREATION

Everything was created by God. A little boy was once asked if he knew what 'to create' means. 'Yes,' he said, 'to make something out of nothing.' It was a good answer.

If a man is making a table, what does he need? Wood, nails, glue, tools. If a woman is making a cake, what does she need? Flour, sugar, butter, eggs, a cooker. God made everything out of nothing. That is creation.

It was an easy thing for God to create all things. He did it simply by speaking. The Bible tells us, 'He spoke, and it was done.' So in the book of Genesis ('the book of beginnings') we keep reading: 'And God said, Let there be . . . And it was so.'

God created everything in six days.

1. Light.
2. Air and clouds.
3. Dry land and things that grow.
4. Sun, moon, and stars.
5. Sea creatures and birds.
6. Land animals and man.

It happened immediately when God commanded. And there were no mistakes; there was no need to have a number of tries. Everything was perfect.

The seventh day God rested. That is why He gave the Sabbath day (one day in seven) as a day of rest in which we cease from work and play. Why do we now keep Sunday instead of Saturday? Because it is the day when

Jesus rose from the dead and in the days of the Apostles the day was changed from the seventh to the first. The important thing from the beginning was one day in seven.

As most children know, some people do not believe that God created the world. They think it just happened. A famous German mathematician, Athanasius Kircher, once had such a person come to see him. He placed a beautiful globe of the world in a corner of the room so that his visitor could not help seeing it. Very soon the visitor asked: 'Where did you get that beautiful globe? Whoever made it?'

'No one,' said Kircher, 'it just happened.'

The other man, of course, was amazed at this answer and just stared at him.

'Well,' said the famous mathematician, 'you are amazed if someone suggests this little globe just happened, and yet how can you think such a thing of this great and beautiful world?'

At school you may be taught that man was not created but that he came from animals. This is known as *Evolution*. The Bible clearly tells us that God created Adam from the dust of the ground, and Eve from Adam's side. We cannot, of course, in a little book like this try to answer all the attacks on the Bible account of creation, but we just mention a few things:

1. Evolution is just a theory; it has never been proved. Many famous scientists are (and have been) Christians and believe fully in the Bible account of creation.

2. The Bible is not a science book, and we agree that a lot more could be said. But there is no mistake. There is nothing contrary to true science. A true scientist's work is to *observe*, to write about what has been observed, and to

make deductions from that. It is the place of the historian to write what has taken place. No scientist was there to observe creation. But God was.

3. We do not see evolution taking place now. Better-quality horses may be bred, but we do not see a horse changing into a cow, or a pig into a sheep.

People in all ages, in all cultures, in different countries have been able to understand the beautiful account of creation. Even little children can understand it. How great God is! How beautiful the world He has made! How kind a Creator!

And how wonderful that we can speak to this great Creator in prayer! This great God loves His people. Sometimes on a very starry night they look up with amazement at the heavens: 'When I consider the heavens, which Thou hast made, the moon and stars, the work of Thy fingers, what is man? . . . ' And they feel, 'This great God is my Saviour and my Friend.'

Suggested Bible readings
   Genesis 1.
   Genesis 2.
   Psalm 8.
   Psalm 33: 1–9.

CHAPTER 4

MAN

The story has often been told of the clock that just would not go. 'Leave it a few days, and see what happens,' was suggested. But still the clock would not go. 'It needs oiling well'—so this was tried; but still the clock would not go. All kinds of things were tried: 'Give it a good shake'; 'Put it in a different place', etc. At last it was taken to the shop where it was bought. 'We shall have to send it back to the makers,' they said. It came back from the makers with just one comment: 'IT NEEDS A NEW INSIDE. THE SPRING IS BROKEN.'

What a picture of man! We read of dreadful things—crime, murder, violence, burglary, etc., and all kinds of ways are used to try to stop them—education, more schools, more police, remand homes, detention centres—but man remains as bad as ever! Why? Because he is wrong at heart; his mind, and will, and affections, and understanding are completely wrong. He is a sinner.

The Bible word is that man is *fallen*. He was not always as he is. God made man perfect. He made him out of the dust of the earth. He gave him a soul. He made him different from all the animals. In the Garden of Eden we see man unfallen and happy, peaceful, enjoying union with his Maker.

Then the Fall. A little boy, when asked what the Fall meant, gave a good but simple answer: 'Adam fell from good to bad.' We all fell in Adam; Adam is the 'head of us all'. You remember when Goliath and David fought,

Goliath said, 'Don't let the two armies fight. You choose a man to fight for you; I will fight for the Philistines.' David was the 'head' of the Israelites (the Israelites were 'in him'); Goliath was the 'head' of the Philistines (all the Philistines were 'in him'). David won, so all Israel won; Goliath lost, so all the Philistines lost. We were *in* Adam; we fought, we lost, we fell. So 'sin entered the world, and death by sin; and so death passed upon all men for that all have sinned'. This is the doctrine of 'original sin'.

We are born into this world as sinners, our hearts are depraved, and so as we grow up we sin in word, thought, and deed. We do not love the Lord with all our heart, mind, soul, and strength. *We are not sinners because we sin. We sin because we are sinners.* 'Sin is the transgression of God's law.' God has given us a good, holy law—the ten commandments. We break them. We are guilty. We deserve eternal punishment.

Because we have sinned we must die (and after death there is the judgement). 'The wages of sin is death.' Some years ago plans were drawn up for a beautiful new town—an *ideal* town.

'But where is the police station?' a visitor asked.

With a smile he was answered, 'There will be no need for any police in this lovely environment.'

'But there is no church,' persisted the visitor.

Again a smile: 'No one will want to go to church when the time comes for the town to be built.'

The visitor, however, did not give up. 'Why is there no cemetery?'

Silence! No answer to this question!

We can do nothing to save ourselves. We cannot deliver ourselves. We are helpless and guilty. We are like

14

the clock—we need a new inside. The story is told of the little black boy who fell into a pit. Night, with all the dangers of wild beasts, drew nearer, and he could not get out. He trembled with fear. A crowd of natives gathered round. One told him he was a foolish boy to fall in. Another said he was very naughty to be playing near the hole. A third told him to get out as he got in (which he could not). Another threw him a stick to hold, but the stick broke. Of all things, someone even lectured him that when he did get out, he must never fall in again! And the night grew nearer—until at length a very strong, kind native went right down into the pit himself, picked him up, and lifted him out.

Our need is so great we need the Lord Jesus to do *everything* for us.

Some of you will have heard the story of 'The Little Highland Maid'. A well-known Scottish minister was conducting worship in the house where he was staying. He asked if all were present. 'Yes,' they said, 'apart from a little maid. She is in the kitchen. She will not understand. She cannot read or write.'

The minister insisted that the little girl was brought. When he asked her questions, it was clear that she did not know the first thing about religion. Before he left, the minister taught her to pray this prayer: 'LORD, SHOW ME MYSELF.'

Later, when the minister again visited that home, he found the maid in great trouble and distress. Asking the cause, he found she was burdened with a sense of her sin and guilt before a holy God. Her prayer had been answered. Now he talked to her about the Lord Jesus, and left her with another prayer: 'LORD, SHOW ME THYSELF.'

Not until many years after did the two meet again. It was a gracious young lady, rejoicing in God's salvation, who introduced herself to the minister, and told him how the second prayer had been answered, and Jesus made precious to her as her Saviour.

Suggested Bible readings
  Genesis 3.
  Romans 1: 18–32.
  Romans 3: 9–20, 23.

CHAPTER 5

THE PERSON OF CHRIST

When the Lord Jesus rode on a donkey into Jerusalem, the people asked an important question. They said, 'WHO IS THIS?' We do need to know the answer. Who was Jesus? Who is Jesus?

1. *He was not an ordinary man*. He was (and is) God. He is almighty. He can do anything.

Before He ever came to Earth, before ever He was born at Bethlehem, He lived as God in Heaven. Two children's hymns are very helpful:

> He came down to earth from Heaven,
>   Who is God and Lord of all.

> Jesus, who lived above the sky,
>   Came down to be a Man, and die.

2. *He was a real Man*. He was born. Though He had no human father, He had a human mother, Mary. He was hungry. He felt pain. He was weary (on the well at Samaria). He cried (at Lazarus' grave). He was asleep (at the back of the ship).

3. *He was completely free from sin*. The Bible says, 'Holy, harmless, undefiled, separate from sinners' (Hebrews 7: 26). He never did, or said, or thought anything that was wrong.

He could be tempted but could not sin ('impeccable'); His human life never existed apart from His being God.

When we are tempted, we often sin. We are like those lovely rock pools by the sea; they seem so clear, but if you take a stick and stir the bottom they are immediately cloudy and dark. Not so the Lord Jesus. When Satan came with his stick to stir, there was nothing for him to work on.

Pilate tried hard, but he could 'find no fault in the Man'.

The Roman soldier by the cross said, 'Certainly this was a righteous Man.'

Even Satan can find no flaw, no fault.

When God the Father looks down from Heaven He says, 'This is My beloved Son, in whom I am well pleased.' His dear Son has perfectly fulfilled His law.

Girls and boys sometimes ask: '*How can we be sure that Jesus is God?*'

1. Well, there are lots of passages that clearly tell us He is ('the Bible tells me so'). For instance, 'In the beginning was the Word [i.e. the Lord Jesus], and the Word was with God, and the Word was God' (John 1: 1). 'Christ came, who is over all, God blessed for ever' (Romans 9: 5). 'But unto the Son He saith, Thy throne, O God, is for ever and ever' (Hebrews 1: 8).

A man once asked the question, 'If Jesus is truly God, why doesn't the Bible say so?'

He was asked in return exactly what he would like it to say.

'Something like, "This is the true God".'

He was immediately shown 1 John 5: 20—speaking of Jesus—'*This is the true God.*'

2. But then:

Jesus is to be worshipped—and we must worship only God. We are to pray to Him—and we can pray to none

18

but God. He performed wonderful miracles—as a proof that He is God. His resurrection is a proof that He is God—only a man that is God can rise by His own power.

Some girls and boys can say:

> That Christ is God I can avouch,
> And for His people cares;
> For I have prayed to Him as such,
> And He has heard my prayers.

Though Jesus died, He rose again, and then went back up into Heaven. He is there—still a real Man, but now for ever 'crowned with glory and honour'.

Some people say, 'I believe that Jesus was a good Man, but I cannot believe He was God.' Well, it must be one or the other; it cannot be both. After all that Jesus said, claiming to be who He is, if He is *not* God, then He cannot be a *good* Man.

Like the wise men we would come with another question: 'WHERE IS HE?' We want to find Him, and know Him, to worship and to love Him.

WHAT THINK YE OF CHRIST?

Suggested Bible readings

Matthew 1: 18–25, and chapter 2 give an account of the birth of Jesus, and also Luke 1: 26–38, and chapter 2.

Read also Psalms 45 and 72, John 1: 1–14, and Hebrews 1 and 2.

Wherever you read in the Gospel according to John you will find he stresses that Jesus is God.

CHAPTER 6

THE HOLY SPIRIT

There used to be a little poem that many children learned at school:

> Who has seen the wind?
> Neither you nor I.

In the Bible the Holy Spirit is compared to the wind. You cannot *see* the wind blowing but on a windy day you can see the effects. A hat blowing down the street; smoke swirling; dustbin lids being blown away. The wind has tremendous power; we sometimes even read of a car being blown off the motorway.

But there are two things we must always remember; two things which are often forgotten:

1. *The Holy Spirit is a Person*—not just a feeling or an influence. This is very important.

In the Bible many things are said about the Holy Spirit which could only be said of a person. (It is wrong to speak of the Holy Spirit as 'it'.) For instance:

He loves—Romans 15: 30.
He is grieved—Ephesians 4: 30.
He can be lied to—Acts 5: 3.
He reproves—John 16: 8.
He gives—1 Corinthians 12: 8–11.
He is a witness—1 John 5: 7.
He knows—1 Corinthians 2: 11; 12: 8; John 14: 26.
He can be sinned against—Matt. 12: 32, 33.

2. *The Holy Spirit is a Divine Person*. He is God. He is

eternal. He knows everything ('omniscient'). He is almighty ('omnipotent'). He is everywhere ('omnipresent').

At the end of each service you hear the minister speak the words of the benediction: 'The grace of the Lord Jesus Christ, and the love of God, and the communion of the Holy Ghost. . . .' There God the Holy Spirit is joined with God the Father and with God the Son—one God.

When a person is baptized, he is baptized 'in the name (*not* "names") of the Father, and of the Son, and of the Holy Ghost'. Again God the Holy Ghost is joined with God the Father and God the Son.

But also we are warned of *blasphemy* against the Holy Ghost. Now only a Person who is God can be blasphemed. If you say awful things against the mightiest ruler or the holiest minister, it is wicked—but it is not blasphemy. 'All manner of sin and blasphemy shall be forgiven unto men: but the blasphemy against the Holy Ghost shall not be forgiven unto men' (Matthew 12: 31).

Then, too, we may *pray* to the Holy Spirit, and, of course, that would be sinful if He were not God.

You all know the solemn story of Ananias and Sapphira (Acts 5), how they were both punished with death for telling a lie. Verse 3 tells us clearly they lied 'to the Holy Ghost'; verse 4 adds: 'Thou hast not lied unto men, but *unto God*.'

Many names are given to the Holy Spirit. He is sometimes spoken of as the holy Dove, or the heavenly Dove—the thought being of His appearance at the baptism of the Lord Jesus; He is the divine Comforter; He is often spoken of as 'the Holy Ghost' as well as 'the Holy Spirit'. 'Ghost' is a very old word for spirit.

(Four hundred years ago a minister would be spoken of as 'your ghostly teacher'.)

Is there any difference at all between 'the Holy Ghost' and 'the Holy Spirit'? No. None at all. The same word is translated sometimes by the one word, and sometimes by the other.

The happening we usually think of in connection with the Holy Spirit is the Day of Pentecost. In Acts 2 we have a description of how the Holy Spirit came down (like tongues of fire) on the disciples and how, as they preached with power, 3000 people were 'pricked in their hearts' (by the Holy Spirit), repented, believed on the Lord Jesus, and were baptized. 'And they continued stedfastly.'

Let us be clear. The Day of Pentecost was not the beginning of the Holy Spirit (any more than the birth of Jesus was *His* beginning). There never was a time when there was not the Holy Spirit; He was there at creation; He was there before creation. The Day of Pentecost was the time when, in a special way, He displayed His almighty power.

The Holy Spirit as well as being active in creation was also active in the resurrection of the Lord Jesus. But there are three special works of the Holy Spirit:

1. *The birth of the Lord Jesus.* How was it possible that Jesus should be born of a virgin? Mary herself asked, 'How can these things be?' The answer given by the angel was: 'The Holy Ghost shall come upon thee, and the power of the Highest shall overshadow thee; therefore that holy thing which shall be born of thee shall be called the Son of God' (Luke 1: 35).

We do not try to explain it; we believe it.

22

2. *The inspiration of the Bible.* 'Holy men of old wrote as they were moved by the Holy Ghost' (2 Peter 1: 21).

3. *The work of grace in the heart.* We know nothing until the Holy Spirit works in our hearts in the new birth. This is completely His work, giving divine life.

Then He carries on the work He has begun. He leads. He teaches. He helps in prayer. He comforts. He unfolds the Scriptures. He reveals Jesus.

We sorely need the Holy Spirit to work in us continually. We know nothing without Him.

What a mercy it is that the Lord Jesus encourages us to pray for the gift of the Holy Spirit! He takes the example of a kind father and asks the question: if a little child wants a piece of bread because he is hungry, would his father give him a stone? Or if it was some fish he asked for, do you think it possible he would give him a snake? Or again, if this time he asked for an egg, what would you say if the father instead gave him a stinging scorpion? Then these beautiful words follow:

'If ye then, being evil, know how to give good gifts unto your children: *how much more* shall your heavenly Father give the Holy Spirit to them that ask Him?' (Luke 11: 13).

Suggested Bible readings
    John 14: 16–27.
    John 16: 6–15.
    Acts 2 (the Day of Pentecost).

CHAPTER 7

ELECTION

Girls and boys often hear the word 'election' and perhaps are bewildered by it. Or at school people say, 'You believe in election at your chapel.' Well, we do. Whatever people may say, the Bible is full of election. I remember years ago a boy, who fully believed the Bible to be God's Word, saying to me, 'I just do *not* believe in election.' 'Well,' I said, 'read Romans chapter 9.' He did; and said, 'I admit I cannot understand it, but it is there, very clearly.'

What is election? Before God made the world He knew that men would sin and so deserve His punishment. But in love God chose certain persons out of the human race and decreed that they would be saved from sin, and at last go to heaven.

We see this worked out right through the Bible. There were many people living in Ur; but God spoke to one man, Abraham. Abraham had two sons, Isaac and Ishmael; but Isaac was chosen. Isaac had two sons, Jacob and Esau; but Jacob was chosen.

It has always been so. For instance, in the Black Country district years ago lived two boys. Both were the same age. Both were in the same class. Both were called George Rose. They had to be known as George Rose 'A' and George Rose 'B'. After leaving school they lost sight of each other for many years. One day they met. One George Rose was going to the greyhound track; the other George Rose was going to preach.

People usually say, 'But this is unfair!' The way the

Bible reveals it is rather this: if God had willed, He might have chosen *none*, He might have punished *all*. None, of themselves, would choose God. Election does not shut any out: their sin has done that; it shuts millions in.

The Bible always speaks of election as an *election of grace*—the wonderful grace of Almighty God in choosing sinners that they might at last go to heaven. A famous American preacher was once asked: 'WHAT IS GRACE?' He gave the following reply. If a tramp came to my house and I gave him a lovely meal and then a comfortable bed for the night, that would be *kindness*. But if that tramp were to steal some of my valuable possessions and then again, the next night, I gave him a lovely meal and comfortable bed, that would be *grace*. ('Grace is God's free favour in the face of active demerit.')

A girl or boy may ask, 'How may I know if I am elect?' God in His Word always joins together *election* and *calling*. 'All that the Father giveth Me' (election), says Jesus, 'shall come to Me' (calling) (John 6: 37). 'Blessed is the man whom Thou choosest' (election) 'and causest to approach unto Thee' (calling) (Psalm 65: 4). Those that God chose in eternity He calls in time. One by one they are brought to feel their need of the Lord Jesus, and come to Him for salvation. And each needy sinner is invited and welcome. 'Come unto Me, all ye that labour and are heavy laden, and I will give you rest.'

So the command is: 'Give diligence to make your *calling* and *election* sure' (in that order) (2 Peter 1: 10). Am I called by God's grace? Has He taught me my need as a sinner? Have I had to venture on the Lord Jesus? Is He my only hope? Then if *called* I am *chosen* (elect).

The best explanation we have ever heard is this. In

Scotland a few godly people were seeking to answer the question: 'How may I know that God has chosen me? How may I know that I am one of the elect?' At length an old soldier was asked to speak. This is what he said:

You all know that I am an old soldier. Because of this every month I receive a pension. Now I believe that in London there is a big book where are written the names of every old soldier receiving the pension. I have never been to London. I have never seen the book, or read my name there. But because month by month the pension comes, I know my name must be there.

He continued: So, I believe there is a book in heaven, the Lamb's book of life, with all the names of the elect. I have never been up to heaven. I have not seen the book, nor read my name there. But because from time to time divine favours flow down from heaven into my soul, I know my name must be written there.

> The streams of love I trace
>   Back to their fountain God;
> And in His wondrous mercy see
> Eternal thoughts of love to me.

Suggested Bible readings
   Romans 8: 28–39.
   Romans 9: 6–24.
   Ephesians 1, especially the first part.

CHAPTER 8

REDEMPTION

Years ago, in a far-off land, a number of beautiful birds
were for sale. From the large cage where they were kept
they tried to escape, but they could not. One day along
came a distinguished-looking man. He asked how much
the birds cost. Then to everyone's astonishment he said he
wished to buy them all. But the people were more amazed
when, having paid the price, he opened the cage door and
let them all fly away. (He said, 'I was once in prison!')

That is redemption. Redemption means 'to set free by
paying a price'. The man paid the price. The birds were
rightly his. Then he set them free.

The Lord Jesus came from Heaven to Earth to *redeem*
His people (those God had chosen). They were prisoners
to sin and Satan. He came to set them free. The children's
hymn explains it very beautifully:

> There was no other good enough
>   To pay the price of sin;
> He only could unlock the gates
>   Of Heaven, and let us in.

The Lord Jesus redeemed His people by dying for them.
By His death He paid the price. Have you noticed what
a large part of the gospels is taken up with the story of the
death of the Lord Jesus? He came to tell men about God;
He came to teach; He came to set a good example. But
especially He came to die.

Many children cannot understand why God could not
forgive His people their sins without His dear Son having

27

to die such a cruel death on the cross. We remember a minister years ago speaking on the text: 'In whom we have redemption through His blood, even the forgiveness of sins' (Ephesians 1: 7). He spoke of when he was a boy. One day he was carrying a long plank when someone shouted, 'George!' He quickly turned round, and the plank smashed through a window. Immediately he ran to his father and said, 'Do please forgive me. I'm sorry!'

'Of course I'll forgive you,' said his father, 'but someone will have to pay for the window!'

God does not forgive without His holiness, His justice being satisfied. But how was God's justice satisfied when Jesus died? You may ask, 'What can the Lord Jesus dying on the cross have to do with sin being forgiven, or taken away?'

There is an old story of two boys who were close friends. As they grew older they went different ways, and then for years did not see each other at all. One day they met again—in strange circumstances. One was the judge. The other was the criminal in the dock. The case was heard and the criminal was clearly guilty. What could the judge do? Could he say it did not matter because it was his friend? No true judge would do that. So an interesting thing took place. The judge pronounced the criminal guilty. He stated the heavy fine that he had to pay (and the poor man had no money to pay it). Then the judge left his seat, went and stood by his old friend, the criminal, and said, 'I'll pay the fine for you.' So the judge himself paid the fine, and the criminal went free.

Sin must be punished. But the Lord Jesus so dearly loved His people that He paid their debt, He bore their punishment, He died *in their place* (a substitute).

> He saw how wicked men had been,
> He knew that God must punish sin,
> So, for His people, Jesus said
> He'd bear the punishment instead.

That is redemption—the only way of salvation, the only way to Heaven.

So we think of the wonderful love of the Lord Jesus in dying for His people. We think of the awful sorrows He endured when He was nailed to the cross. We think of His greater sorrows, feeling the weight of His people's sins and His Father's anger. And we know that in shedding His precious blood, He for ever took His people's sins away. He died that they might live.

Suggested Bible readings

The different accounts of the death of the Lord Jesus: Matthew 26 and 27; Mark 14 and 15; Luke 22 and 23; John 18 and 19.

Read also Isaiah 53 and almost anywhere in the Epistle to the Hebrews.

CHAPTER 9

THE RESURRECTION

Some years ago a young man was preaching the gospel. One of his hearers, an atheist, passed up a note to him: 'What has your religion got that all these other religions have not got?' and underneath there was a long list: Buddhism, Mohammedanism, Confucianism, Hinduism, Marxism, etc.

The young man paused for a moment; then wrote an answer to the question: 'AN EMPTY TOMB'.

We have this wonderful fact—apart from people's beliefs or feelings—the fact that 'the Lord is risen indeed'. Someone once said the resurrection is 'the best attested fact of history'. Be that as it may, there is certainly as much (or more) proof of the resurrection of Jesus as there is of the coming of Julius Caesar to Britain in 55 BC.

You all know the story of how Jesus rose from the dead—His lifeless body laid in the grave; the heavy stone; the guard of soldiers; then the angel from heaven rolling away the stone and the Lord Jesus triumphantly coming back to life and leaving the grave. No doubt you can remember how He appeared:

1. To Mary Magdalene.
2. To the women coming back from the grave.
3. To Peter.
4. To the two on the way to Emmaus.
5. To the disciples in the upper room.
6. To Thomas (and the other disciples).
7. To the disciples by the Sea of Galilee.

8. On a mountain to 500.
9. To James.
10. To the disciples before ascending.

If someone tells us a strange piece of news which we can hardly believe, we always think, 'Can I really trust him?' Well, can we really trust the accounts we have of Jesus' rising? We answer with an emphatic 'YES'. Why?

1. The writers were honourable men, men who always spoke the truth, men who can be relied on, men always counted as 'saints'. They were men who were willing to *die* for what they believed because they were so certain of it.

2. You cannot help seeing the difference in these men. We read of how, when Jesus was crucified, they 'all forsook Him and fled'. Peter was so afraid that He even cursed and swore, saying that He did not know Jesus. We see them, afraid, in that upper room, the doors locked. A little later they are brave, courageous; they are not afraid to stand up before their enemies. Their preaching is believed by multitudes. What had made the difference in that little time? Had something happened? Yes, their Lord and Master, whom they had seen crucified, had come back to life and they had seen Him and talked with Him.

3. If Jesus did *not* rise from the dead, why did His enemies not produce His body? When Peter preached on the Day of Pentecost (six weeks later) saying that Jesus was alive, His grave was close at hand. But no one could go there and say, 'Here is His body.' No, 'He is not here; He is risen, as He said.'

There is an interesting book, written by a man named Frank Morison. Its title is *Who Moved the Stone?* Frank

Morison thought it silly that people should believe that Jesus rose from the dead so he sat down to write a book to prove how ridiculous it all was. First he tried to gather his evidence together. But the harder he tried, the more he became sure that Jesus did rise from the dead. In the end the book he wrote was the *opposite* of the one he tried to write! It begins with a chapter about 'the book which refused to be written'!

Some girls and boys seem to be worried about the different accounts given by Matthew, Mark, Luke, and John. Why are they so different? Well, there must have been an awful lot of 'coming and going' on the resurrection morning. One tells of one thing; another of something else. *But they do not contradict one another.* Three children, after going out to tea, are asked what they had to eat. One says, 'jelly'; the second, 'sausage rolls'; the third, 'birthday cake'. They are all perfectly truthful!

Why is the resurrection so important? Elijah raised a little boy; so did Elisha. What is different in the resurrection of Jesus? Well, they did it by the power of God, Jesus by His own power. Those whom they raised one day died, but Jesus rose, never to die again. And the Lord Jesus had *said* that He would die, *said* that He would rise again.

His rising proved that He is what He said—the Son of God. His rising proved that God had accepted the sacrifice He offered. His rising shows that one day the bodies of all His people (as well as the wicked) shall rise. The Bible speaks of it as 'the firstfruits'. In ancient Israel one sheaf of corn was taken from the harvest field and offered to the Lord. This was the firstfruits. But it was a pledge that as the firstfruits were safely gathered in, so the whole harvest would be soon. 'Now is Christ risen from the dead, and become the firstfruits of them that slept' (1 Corinthians 15: 20).

We read that Jesus 'was raised for our justification'. ('To justify' is a legal term: God declaring His people just, because of what Jesus has done.) You may say, 'But was it not when Jesus *died* that His people were saved?' Yes, most surely it was. But if you were sentenced to prison for a debt, and someone went to prison for you, when would you rejoice? When you saw him go into prison, or while he lay there, or when he came out? Would you not be happy when you saw the prison doors open and your friend go free? It was his time in prison that paid your debt; but when he came forth out of prison, you knew that your debt was completely paid and now you were free.

The Lord Jesus, forty days after rising from the dead, ascended into heaven. There He lives and reigns. He has died, entered the grave, but has come out. The old story used to be told of a lion luring his victims to his cave with fair promises, until one said, 'No, all the footsteps go *in*; none come *out*.' And people say of the grave, 'But all the footsteps go *in*.' In the dear Lord Jesus we see footsteps coming *out*.

The great thing is to *know* the Lord Jesus. The old preachers used to speak of 'a once-crucified but now risen and exalted Jesus'. He is the only way to heaven. That is a good prayer of Paul's: 'That I may know Him.' Not just know *about* Him, but know Him, personally. (What a difference there is between *knowing* a person and just knowing *about* him! Everyone knows *about* the Queen; few actually know her.)

Over the years many girls and boys have prayed that beautiful prayer:

> Lord Jesus, make Thyself to me
> A living, bright reality!
> More present to faith's vision keen
> Than any outward object seen,
> More dear, more intimately nigh
> Than e'en the sweetest earthly tie.

Suggested Bible readings

The different accounts of the resurrection: Matthew 28; Mark 16; Luke 24; John 20–21.

Read also 1 Corinthians 15.

CHAPTER 10

THE NEW BIRTH

A few years ago I noticed a very strange thing whilst sitting in the pulpit. The chapel clock was going the wrong way round! The service started at seven, but by the time we had sung the first hymn it was five to seven! and at the end of the Bible reading it was a quarter to seven! At first I wondered if my eyes were playing tricks and even came down from the pulpit to ask!

That clock had been going round in one direction only, day after day, week after week, year after year. But now suddenly, unexpectedly, it started going round completely the opposite way. I began to think. That is what we see happening in the lives of men and women, girls and boys—A COMPLETE CHANGE. We have it in the Bible with some who were very wicked—we think of Manasseh and Mary Magdalene.

Sometimes it is called *conversion*: 'Except ye be converted and become as little children ye cannot see the kingdom of heaven.' It is God's work, not man's; not just turning over a new leaf, not just reforming, not just giving up some sinful habit. The chapel clock soon went back to its old ways, but a true conversion continues. On the Day of Pentecost there were 3000 and they all 'continued stedfastly'.

A godly minister was once walking down the street and his attention was drawn to a drunkard lying in the gutter.

'There is one of your converts!' someone called.

'Yes,' replied the minister, 'it looks like my work. If it had been God's work, he would not be lying there!'

The Bible also speaks of *the new birth*, the giving of a new life, life from God in the heart. It is this that causes the conversion, the turning round. So the new birth (*regeneration* it is sometimes called) must come before everything else. A baby is born; then it begins to cry, hunger, thirst, move, etc. When we are born again, we begin to hunger and thirst after Christ, and to move in different ways.

As this is completely God's work, it does not matter how bad the person was before. There are countless stories of most wicked persons whose hearts and lives have been changed by God's grace. A man once went to hear George Whitefield preach, carrying several stones to throw at his head during the sermon. But as the sermon began, the stones one by one were dropped on the floor. (Instead of the man breaking Whitefield's *head*, God broke the man's *heart*.) Another time a man climbed on a table in a public house to mimic Whitefield's preaching; but as he spoke his own words affected his heart, and he fled from the place in deep sorrow of soul. He became a godly man and a minister.

The Lord Jesus clearly preached the new birth and the point He insisted on was that it is *vital*. There is no substitute for it. We often go into a shop and are told, 'We don't have what you want, but we have something that is just as good.' There is no substitute for the new birth.

Nicodemus, who was a ruler among the Jews (we might say, a Member of Parliament), came to Jesus secretly by night. Outwardly he was a good man, a religious man, and he spoke so kindly to the Lord Jesus. But Jesus came straight to the point: 'Ye must be born again.' No salvation without it! In other words: Nicodemus all your religion and good works will not do. You are wrong at heart. You need that complete change, that new life that only God can give.

The important thing in the change is new life. Often in the Bible it is compared to a *resurrection*. What Jesus did for Jairus' daughter, Lazarus, and the widow of Nain's son, we need Him to do for us. Sometimes going into a house we notice a beautiful display of colourful flowers. On going up to them, though, we find they are artificial. There is no life. We do not want to be like the artificial flowers.

Where there is this life given, this change, we *repent* and *believe*. There is so much in the Bible about repentance and faith.

We need to repent because of our sin, our disobedience, our rebellion against God. Jesus preached that 'men ought to repent'. So John the Baptist preached repentance, and the Apostles preached repentance. It is very clear that there is no forgiveness without repentance.

What is repentance? To be sorry for our sins and turn from them to God. It is a turning round (like the clock). How we need to be sorry for all our sins, and to confess them! But what good is it if we even weep about our sins, and still go on the same? The little children's hymn is very much to the point:

> Repentance is to leave
>   The sins we loved before,
> And show that we in earnest grieve
>   By doing them no more.

We well remember an old man, a ruffian, well known

in the town, who came to chapel once a year at the anniversary. Throughout the service he would weep, and at the end would say, 'I know this is where I should be! I know this is where I should be!' Then we would not see him for another year. One year he was not there; he had taken his own life. Tears, however many, without forsaking sin—that is not repentance.

Then there is *faith*. This is not just to believe that Jesus lived, and died, and rose again, but to *trust* Him. And both repentance and faith are the gift of God. Where there is real conversion, where the new birth takes place, then we renounce any hope in ourselves, or any confidence in what we have done, and trust ONLY in the Lord Jesus.

How important that little word *only* is! At the time of the Reformation the great debate between Protestants and Roman Catholics was about justification by faith. But the Roman Catholics were willing to agree to justification by faith—so long as the word 'only' or 'alone' was left out. 'Be sure you don't give up that word *only*,' was the advice given to a few ministers as they journeyed to a debate with their opponents.

Faith is personal and there is always that element of trust in it. How much there is in the story of Blondin, the famous tightrope walker! He could walk blindfold across a tightrope stretched over the Niagara Falls. He could even push a man across in a wheelbarrow, unbelievable as it seems! On one occasion he was talking to a friend about his achievements. He asked the friend if he really believed that he could push a man safely across. 'Yes,' said his friend. Blondin pressed him on this point as to whether he really believed it would be safe.

'I have no doubt at all, from what I know of your ability, of the man's safety.'

But he would not climb into the wheelbarrow! He did not really trust him!

How important is the Holy Spirit's work in the new birth, enabling us to turn from sin to God, and to trust the Lord Jesus!

To quote Whitefield once more: he was once staying at a house where he was treated with the greatest courtesy and kindness. However, sadly, he could see they were strangers to the new birth. Praying as to how he could deal with the matter, he picked up a diamond ring and wrote on the mirror, 'YET ONE THING THOU LACKEST', and God made that word a blessing.

On one occasion the Lord Jesus was asked, 'Are there few that be saved?' They just wanted to satisfy their curiosity: 'Are there few that be saved?' Jesus answered their question, but not as they expected: 'Strive to enter in at the strait gate.' In other words: What about *yourself*?

'One thing is needful' (Luke 10: 42).

'Ye must be born again' (John 3: 7).

'Except a man be born of water and the Spirit, he cannot enter into the kingdom of God' (John 3: 5).

'Except ye be converted, and become as little children, ye shall not enter into the kingdom of heaven' (Matthew 18: 3).

'Except ye repent ye shall all likewise perish' (Luke 13: 3, 5).

Suggested Bible readings
   John 3: 1–17.
   Ephesians 2: 1–9.

39

CHAPTER 11

SANCTIFICATION

We often read in the paper about people being sent to prison. Perhaps they have been stealing, or it may even be that they have killed someone. The sad thing is that when they come out of prison they are no better, no different from what they were before. How often we read of a person committing some crime the very day he was set free from prison!

Now when God forgives a person it is not like that. When God forgives He makes that person different. From now on his life is completely changed.

The most wicked man in the Bible was the Old Testament king, Manasseh. But one day God began to deal with him; he was in great trouble, and asked God to forgive him. And God did. But from that moment Manasseh's life was different. He stopped doing the bad things he had done and started doing the opposite.

The Bible calls this *sanctification*. Manasseh was not only forgiven but God sanctified him. Every person God saves from going to hell He sanctifies. If a judge forgives someone, he cannot sanctify him; but what men cannot do, what the law cannot do, God does.

To sanctify something really means to set it apart for some holy use. In the tabernacle and temple in the Old Testament, cups and basons were 'sanctified'; they were set apart to be used *only* in the services, they were not to be used for ordinary things. God set apart His people before they were born, but when they are born again they are actually sanctified—made holy in heart and conduct.

The little children's hymn says: 'He died that we might be forgiven'—that is salvation; 'He died to make us good'—that is sanctification. The grace that saves also sanctifies.

Many girls and boys mix up justification and sanctification; so do many older people. If we are God's people,

Justification	*Sanctification*
is outside us	is within us
is perfect	is not perfect
counts us holy	makes us holy
is our standing	is our experience
saves us from sin's guilt	saves us from sin's power.

We need the work of the Lord Jesus for us (justification) and the work of the Holy Spirit in us (sanctification).

The Roman Catholics seem to have no doctrine of sanctification. A man sins; then goes to the Mass, partakes of the wafer, and may even have 'holy feelings'; then perhaps he goes out and does the same sins again. But if God's people are saved they must be sanctified. This is what people notice—even ungodly people. They do not read the Bible; they cannot understand some of the doctrines of the Bible; but they do understand when a wicked man begins to behave differently: when a drunken man becomes sober; when a man who has ill-treated his wife becomes kind; when a foul-mouthed man stops swearing; when a dishonest man becomes honest.

Even if people have not been outwardly wicked, yet still

41

there will be a difference. A little servant girl was once asked if she could prove that her life had been changed, that grace had made a difference. She thought a moment, and then said, 'Yes. Up till recently I used to clean everywhere beautifully if it was where people could see; but now the places no one can see are cleaned just as well.'

Sanctification is part of God's work in preparing His people for Heaven. If you took a fish out of the sea to a most beautiful meadow, it could not live. If you plunged an eagle into the depths of a beautiful lake it must die. It would be out of its element. So an unsanctified person could not be happy in Heaven.

We read once of a very poor, ignorant man who inherited a mansion with horse and carriage, beautiful grounds, servants, and untold wealth. (He was a very distant relation, though the next of kin.) But the poor man was miserable. His behaviour was so uncouth that in the end everyone was laughing at him. He had the mansion and the inheritance, but his manners and his nature were unchanged. He was out of his element. Yes, 'Heaven is a prepared place for a prepared people.'

Years ago all Scottish children had to learn their catechism (which they knew as well as their multiplication tables). Every little Scottish girl or boy could answer the question: 'What is sanctification?' — 'Sanctification is the work of God's free grace, whereby we are renewed in the whole man after the image of God, and are enabled . . . to die unto sin, and live unto righteousness.'

But no-one is perfect while still on Earth. There are still the remains of sin in us, and Satan tempts us. So life will be a battle, a hard battle. There are two different natures inside the Christian (like a dog and a cat in one cage). But through God's grace the Christian will win at last—through Christ.

To any girl or boy who feels what it is to struggle and fight, the advice of Scripture is:

Be much in prayer.

Look to Jesus for help.

Depend only on Him.

Distrust your own strength; seek His strength.

Avoid bad places, bad company.

Realize that Satan, the world, and the flesh are stronger than you.

Seek to be kept, daily, hourly.

Pray for grace to stand.

Cling to Christ.

Most of you have heard of John Newton, once a slave dealer and a blasphemer, later called by God's grace and made a minister. John Newton once said: 'I am not what I want to be. I am not what I ought to be. I am not what one day I shall be. BUT I AM NOT WHAT I ONCE WAS.'

Suggested Bible readings

The closing chapters in most of the epistles.

CHAPTER 12

PROVIDENCE

One day a cook poured out a cup of tea for two servant girls. One gladly picked hers up and drank it. The other flung hers right across the room, and immediately cried, 'Oh I am sorry! I don't know why ever I did such a stupid thing!' There was poison in the cup. The girl who had drunk her tea fell dead on the floor.

Why did this happen? People would say it was a lucky chance. But the Bible knows nothing of luck, or chance, or fortune. The Bible, rather, tells us of God's providence. Paul says, 'The things which happened have fallen out unto the furtherance of the gospel' (Philippians 1: 12). They did not just happen. They 'fell out' of God's providence; they 'fell out' as He had planned.

Providence is God ordering everything that ever happens, yet without in any way being responsible for sin. What God planned in eternity (His purpose) He actually does in time (His providence).

Providence touches even the smallest detail in the lives of men, and in all creation. The best little sermon on God's providence is that of the Lord Jesus: 'Are not two sparrows sold for a farthing? and one of them shall not fall on the ground without your Father. But the very hairs of your head are all numbered' (Matthew 10: 29–30).

Not a sparrow can fall to the ground without God ordering it (and the point is: how worthless men count sparrows to be—as we should say, 'two a penny').

If you go home from school and you have lost 10p you

immediately tell your mother, but you do not if you have lost one of your hairs. Well, you probably do not know whether you have or not. But God even knows the number of hairs on our head, and sees when one falls.

> My life's minutest circumstance
> Is subject to Thine eye.

For God's people His providence always works for good. You all know the well-known verse: 'And we know that all things work together for good to them that love God, to them that are the called according to His purpose' (Romans 8: 28).

The Bible in a special way shows God's providence working for good in the Book of Esther. You will have noticed that God's *name* is not mentioned throughout the whole book, but His *hand* can be seen on every page.

Notice how things happened. Haman was going to come before the king the next morning to ask for the death of all the Jews. He specially wanted to be rid of good Mordecai. 'But that night the king could not sleep.' Why *that* night? His bed would be the best and most comfortable. So he sent for the book of the chronicles of what had happened during his reign. Why choose to read a book? Why not something else? And why that special book? And then he read of how Mordecai had saved his life. Why did he turn to *that* page? Then he found that Mordecai had never been rewarded. Why was he never rewarded? And why did the king decide to do it now? How true: 'The king's heart is in the Lord's hand as rivers of water: He turneth it whithersoever He will' (Proverbs 21: 1).

So when wicked Haman next morning came seeking the

lives of the Jews, he found a much different king from the one he had known the day before. 'What shall be done to the man the king delighteth to honour?' asked the king. And it was Mordecai, not Haman, who rode through the city on the king's horse in the king's robes!

Many of you girls and boys will know the wonderful hymn on God's providence:

> God moves in a mysterious way
> His wonders to perform.

The story of Joseph is well known. Everything seemed to be going wrong, yet really everything was going right. His father sent him to visit his brothers, who hated him. But he could not find them. He was about to go back home. But a stranger asked him what he was doing. Why should he ask? And it happened that this particular stranger had heard his brothers say, 'Let us go to Dothan.' Why had he overheard? And why had he remembered? And why should it be their brother he meets? You all know the rest of the story, do you not? Thrown into a pit, sold to the Ishmaelites, a slave to Potiphar, wickedly accused by his mistress, thrown into prison, forgotten . . . until at just the right time God brings him out, he explains Pharaoh's dreams, and Pharaoh makes him the most important person in Egypt. Later he saved the lives of his father and his brothers. He could say to his wicked brothers, 'You meant it for evil, but God meant it for good' (Genesis 50: 20). This is God's providence.

And how much depends on how little! Do you know William Gadsby's verse?

Providence

> There's not a particle of dust can fly,
> A sparrow fall, a cloud obscure the sky,
> A moth be crushed, a leaf fall from a tree,
> But in submission to His wise decree.

Years ago a minister, persecuted because of his religion and hunted by cut-throats, hid in a loft from his enemies. There was nothing to eat and he dare not come out. But each day a hen came where he was hiding and laid an egg for him!

We have mentioned John Newton. He was a man who was never late. But one day, when harbour master at Liverpool, he was late. The boat he was to inspect had gone. But a few minutes later there was an explosion, and it sank!

Augustine (the famous 'St Augustine') always went home the same way. But one day, for some reason, he decided to go another. There were hidden murderers along his usual route waiting to kill him!

A Puritan minister, Mr Dod, one night could not sleep. He felt he *must* go and visit a man in his congregation. His wife told him to go to sleep; at least wait until the morning. 'No,' he said at last, 'I must go now.' And he arrived at the house just as the man was about to kill himself!

At the time of the Reformation Bernard Gilpin was to be put to death for his religion. He was a minister who was always saying, 'All things work together for good to them that love God.' How his enemies laughed when he broke his leg on his way to be killed! They asked, 'How can this work for good?' But it did. Before his leg was healed sufficiently for him to walk to the place of execution, Queen Mary was dead, Queen Elizabeth was reigning, and he was set free.

Perhaps some of you know that over the Royal Exchange in London there is a large grasshopper as the emblem. As a small baby, the founder, Sir Thomas Gresham, was thrown out into a field to die. A little boy passing by heard a grasshopper chirping, and searching for it, found the baby, which his mother nursed and brought up.

During the terrible slaughter of godly people in Paris (the Massacre of St Bartholomew) a minister named Du Moulin crept into an oven to hide. Immediately a spider spun its web over the oven door. 'No use looking in there,' said his cruel enemies.

And hundreds of such stories might be told about the mystery of God's providence, ordering, controlling *everything*.

Suggested Bible readings
   The story of Joseph (Genesis 37–50).
   The Book of Esther, especially the first seven chapters.

CHAPTER 13

ETERNAL SAFETY

Years ago an old man told us his story. When he was young, God had blessed him, and for a time he was very happy. Then, as the days passed, his feelings became dark. He could no longer feel God's blessing. He thought that God had left him, and that he was cast away for ever. Having no one to talk to, and not knowing a good minister, he was completely miserable, thinking he was lost.

One day he sat in church. Sadly he picked up a prayer book (it was Church of England) and without thinking began to turn over its pages. Suddenly, to his amazement, he found he was reading the Thirty-nine Articles and there, for the first time, he read that God never casts away those He has blessed. He has chosen them, predestinated them, Jesus has died for them—so they can never, never be lost. That young man left the church as happy as anyone in England.

Very clearly does the Bible teach this truth—that God's people can never perish. Sometimes they are cast down. Sometimes they are sad. Sometimes they are tempted, and fall. Sometimes they *feel* God has left them. Continually Satan opposes them. But, really, they are safe for ever.

I remember well when one of my little boys went on the train for the first time. Soon after the train had left the station it went over the points. There was a lot of rattling and banging and the little boy in alarm cried, 'We've come off the lines!' But his elder brother had travelled by train before and he quickly assured him, 'No, the train doesn't come off the lines!' So many young Christians, when difficulties and troubles come, think that God has left them, but older ones realize the blessed truth: 'Once in Him, in Him for ever.'

Of course, this should not surprise us. Would a shepherd be happy if one of his sheep were missing? Would a king be happy with one of the jewels missing from his crown? And how can God lose those He has loved and chosen? How can Jesus lose those He has bought at such a cost? How can the Holy Spirit lose those in whose hearts He dwells?

Some have spoken of the three P's:

1. *The promise*. The Lord has promised that His people shall never be cast away, or left to sink into hell at last: 'I give unto them eternal life; and they shall never perish, neither shall any man pluck them out of My hand' (John 10: 28).

2. *The prayer*. The Lord Jesus, before He died, prayed for all His people: that they might be kept and at last go to heaven: 'Father, I will that they also, whom Thou hast given Me, be with Me where I am; that they may behold My glory' (John 17: 24). That prayer *must* be answered.

3. *The power*. We are 'kept by the power of God' (1 Peter 1: 5). The word 'kept' really means 'garrisoned', surrounded by a strong garrison of soldiers. That garrison is the same power that made the world.

The truth that believers can never be lost is a very beautiful one to young persons who belong to Christ. They know how weak they are and how strong Satan is. They realize they may have many years still to live. They feel how severe the fight. But they know that there is safety in Christ. What a miracle that Jesus has never yet lost one, and never will! Young people live in a changing world; everything seems unsure, and often they may feel unsure themselves: but here is something that is certain — every one of God's people will get to heaven.

There are two questions which sometimes puzzle a young person:

'*What about those who seem to be good Christians, and then give it all up?*'

The Bible is very clear on this. There are several who *seemed* to be God's people who perished, e.g. Saul, Ahithophel, Judas Iscariot, Simon Magus, etc. But none of these ever were really the people of God.

But what a solemn warning lest we should only *seem* to be real Christians, and at last prove we were not!

'*Does not the belief "once a child of God always a child of God" lead God's people to live just how they wish and sin as they wish?*'

1. NO! The grace that saves them sanctifies them. The Bible speaks of the lion being changed to the lamb. Among other things there is a change of appetite. You could put a lamb amid a lot of chickens, and it would not eat them all up (as the lion would)!

We remember reading of the young Christian girl who was told by those who used to be her friends that she could no longer do what she wanted. 'Yes, I can,' she said, 'I do what I want.'

'Well, why don't you go dancing, to the cinema?' and a host of other things.

Simply she answered, '*I do not want!*'

2. But if it should be that a child of God does wrong, then God chastises. He makes the person feel sorry and repent—sometimes by His Word; sometimes through trouble.

You have all heard of King David doing wrong—but he did not carry on like that. God made him very, very sorry, and forgave him. A good father does not throw his child out of the house when he does something wrong.

3. The Bible warns about those who do not 'endure to the end'. The proof that we really are God's people is that we do endure.

The well-known John Newton, one time a sea captain, once told of a remarkable dream he had. In his dream he was in Naples harbour when a most glorious person came on board the ship and gave him a precious and beautiful jewel. Thanking him, and taking it from him, John Newton thought there could be no one more happy.

But soon another person came on the deck and began to mock him, saying the jewel was no good, and urging him to throw it away. After a time Newton began to believe him and, taking the jewel, flung it into the sea. Immediately, he was filled with horror. The sky grew dark and the nearby volcano began to erupt. 'Oh! what have I done?' he cried.

After a time the first glorious person came to him again, and asked him about the jewel he had kindly given him. With shame John Newton confessed he had thrown it away. What would happen now? But in his dream he saw the glorious person go over the side of the ship, right down beneath the water, and after a time return with the jewel.

As he came back on the deck, Newton says, 'I held out my hand for it, but he refused. "No," he said, "the jewel is yours; it always will be yours; *but I will keep it for you!*"'

Suggested Bible readings
  John 10.
  John 17.
  Romans 8: 28–39.
  Philippians 1: 1–6.
  1 Peter 1: 1–5.

CHAPTER 14

THE LAST THINGS

Many children are very interested in what will happen at the end of the world. Lots of people are ready to give lots of answers. On things that really matter the Bible is very, very clear.

This world will not go on for ever. One day it will be burned up by fire. God has promised that He will never drown the world again—whenever we see the rainbow in the sky we are reminded of this—but He will one day destroy it by fire.

Where many people have gone wrong—even good people—is in trying to fix a date. In the past all kinds of dates have been suggested; but they have come and gone, and nothing has happened. The year 1870 was one date that various people suggested as the end of the world. Well, girls and boys who enjoy history at school will know that all kinds of important things did happen in 1870; but that is now over a hundred years ago, and the world still goes on.

Lots of guesses do not do any good, especially when the important things are clear. It was the Lord Jesus Himself who spoke so much about the end of the world—and what He has not told us, it is best not to try to find out.

Before the world ends His second coming will take place. He once came as a baby to Bethlehem (His first coming) and He will come again at the end of time (His second coming). Though there are many mysterious things the Lord made four things very clear:

1. *He will come personally.* Just as He bodily ascended into heaven, so bodily, personally He will return to the earth (Acts 1: 11).

2. *He will come in great glory*—not as He once came, a helpless babe, but with all the holy angels with Him (Matthew 24: 30, 31; Mark 13: 26).

3. *His coming will be visible*—everyone will see Him return. It will not be a hidden, secret thing (Luke 17: 24; Revelation 1: 7).

4. *His coming again is certain.* Whatever people say, Jesus will come again (Mark 13: 31; Luke 21: 33).

Many children have heard people talk about 'the millenium'. Whatever is the millenium? The word itself means 'a thousand years', and godly people have been divided in their beliefs about the 'thousand years' (mentioned in Revelation 20).

Some believe that Jesus will come again, and then reign personally on Earth for 1000 years. Then the end of the world will come.

Some believe that there will be 1000 years (or a very long time) of great blessing on Earth; then Jesus will come. Then the world will end.

Some believe there will not be any 1000 years of blessing, but Jesus will come, and that will be the end.

Good people have believed each of the three views but we cannot feel that Jesus will veil His glory a second time to reign personally on Earth. We believe the coming of Jesus will usher in the end of all things, and the judgement day.

At the end of all things, not only will the world be destroyed but all people who have ever lived will be judged. Jesus Himself will be the Judge. Some will still be alive when Jesus comes; those who are dead, righteous and wicked, will rise from the dead—body and soul will be united.

The Lord Jesus as Judge will set all His people on the right hand. He will say to them, 'Come in, ye blessed,' and they will enter Heaven for ever and ever. Heaven is a beautiful place—no sin, no sorrow, no suffering. The glory of heaven is the Lord Jesus Himself. All are perfectly happy.

The rest, on Jesus' left hand, will be cast into hell for ever and ever. Jesus will say, 'Depart, ye cursed.' They will suffer and be in pain; this is the punishment for their sin against God.

Let us be clear. God's people do not go to Heaven because they are any better but because through God's grace they are saved.

A girl or a boy often asks, 'What happens when we die?' Our souls immediately go back to God and enter Heaven or hell; our bodies lie in the grave until the resurrection at the end of time.

You might ask: but what about those whose bodies have been burned, or eaten by wild beasts or cannibals? Our only answer is: what is impossible for us is easy with God. A few pieces of a jigsaw puzzle a little boy can easily gather together; so it is an easy thing for God to gather together every particle of our bodies, whatever has happened to them.

An old lady once had an ugly looking bulb; she put it in the ground, and in the spring there was a beautiful flower. She was reminded that this is the way the Lord speaks of the resurrection of His people (1 Corinthians 15: 35–38; 42–44).

When the Lord Jesus spoke (as He did so often) about the last things—death, His second coming, the end of the world—it was never just to interest people, or amuse them, or to answer silly questions. He always added: 'Be ye therefore ready,' or, 'Watch therefore: for ye know not what hour your Lord doth come.'

A Christian lady had a wicked husband who never went to church or chapel or read the Bible. One day he became most interested in what would happen at the end of the world. He began to spend all day reading the Bible, and his wife was delighted. But, sad to say, his life was no different: he never prayed; he never went to chapel; he went on in his wicked ways. It was just a hobby like gardening or woodwork. We do not want to be like that.

The parables Jesus told (like The Ten Virgins, or The Man Without the Wedding Garment) all clearly teach that *we need to be ready*.

Then what is it to be ready for when Jesus comes—either when we die, or the second coming? Jesus said, 'Ye must be born again.' If you are born again of the Holy Spirit, you will repent, you will be sorry for your sins and turn from them; and you will believe in the Lord Jesus and ask Him to forgive you and take you to heaven. We need the Lord Jesus to *make* us ready, washing us in His precious blood, and clothing us in the wedding garment of His righteousness.

To God's people the second coming will be a most wonderful and blessed time; it will be the time when all God's purposes are complete and He will be glorified for ever and ever.

Years ago a boy had spent much of the weekend talking about the second coming to an old minister who was staying at his house. Much was said and many questions were asked. On the Monday morning the boy took the old man to the station. As his train was pulling in he turned to his young friend and said, 'We have talked a lot about the second coming but the vital thing is to have an interest in His *first* coming.'

> Prepare me, gracious God
> To stand before Thy face . . .
>
> In Christ's obedience clothe,
> And wash me in His blood;
> So shall I lift my head with joy
> Among the sons of God.

Suggested Bible readings
   Matthew 24: 36–42.
   Matthew 25: 1–13.
   1 Thessalonians 4: 13–18.
   Revelation 7: 9–17.
   Revelation 20: 11–15.